Introduction by W. Terrence Gordon

A decade and more before McLuhan came to prominence with The *Gutenberg Galaxy* and *Understanding Media*, he crammed many of their themes into the present essay. It appeared in the inaugural volume of the journal associated with McLuhan's interdisciplinary seminar at the University of Toronto: *Explorations One* (1953). Read today, it illuminates his insights with complementary formulations of themes by key phrases less emphasized or entirely absent from his later writings: posthistoric man, the grammar of gesture, the coherence of the world in latency, the radical imperfection in mechanical media, the inner dialogue or dialectic of print culture. There are fresh analogies: diversity and equilibrium of social awareness assimilated to the body-mind network; fresh metaphors integrating media: "the macadamized surfaces of the printed page," and important precisions: the homogeneity of oral culture is radically different from the homogeneity of print culture. Explicit commentary on language as a medium, a notion unifying McLuhan's thought from *Understanding Media* to his posthumously published *Laws of Media*, is to be found here already. In the age of earth-orbiting satellites, McLuhan would often repeat that they scrapped nature; here, four years before Sputnik opened that era, he states that "the fact that with modern technology the entire material of the globe as well as the thoughts and feelings of its human inhabitants have become the matter of art and of man's factive intelligence means that there is no more nature." McLuhan's orientation to the Symbolist perspective is subtly evoked: "We are all of us persons of divided and sub-divided sensibility through failure to recognize the multiple languages with which our world speaks to us." This is linked to the theme of invisibility of environments, a notion in turn linked to the unity among all media: "[B]ut in respect of this anonymity [of those originating the messages or forms] it is necessary to regard not only words and metaphors as mass media but buildings and cities as well." — WTG

Culture without Literacy

The ordinary desire of everybody to have everybody else think alike with himself has some explosive implications today. The perfection of the *means* of communication has given this average power-complex of the human being an enormous extension of expression.

The telephone, the teleprinter and the wireless made it possible for orders from the highest levels to be given direct to the lowest levels, where, on account of the absolute authority behind them, they were carried out uncritically; or brought it about that numerous offices and command centres were directly connected with the supreme leadership from which they received their sinister orders without any intermediary; or resulted in a widespread surveillance of the citizen, or in a high degree of secrecy surrounding criminal happenings. To the outside observer this governmental apparatus may have resembled the apparently chaotic confusion of lines at a telephone exchange, but like the latter, it could be controlled and operated from one central source. Former dictatorships needed collaborators of high quality even in the lower levels of leadership, men who could think and act independently. In the era of modern technique an authoritarian system can do without this. The means of communication alone permit it to mechanize the work of subordinate leadership. As a consequence a new type develops: the uncritical recipient of orders. [1]

Perfection of the *means* of communication has meant instantaneity. Such an instantaneous network of communication is the body-mind unity of each of us. When a city or a society achieves a diversity and equilibrium of awareness analogous to the body-mind network, it has what we tend to regard as a high culture.

But the instantaneity of communication makes free speech and thought difficult if not impossible and for many reasons. Radio extends the range of the casual speaking voice, but it forbids that many should speak. And when what is said has such range of control it is forbidden to speak any but the most acceptable words and notions. Power and control are in all cases paid for by loss of freedom and flexibility.

Today the entire globe has a unity in point of mutual inter-awareness which exceeds in rapidity the former flow of information in

---

1 Albert Speer, German Armament Minister in 1942, in a speech at the Nuremberg trials, quoted in Hjalmar Schacht, *Account Settled*, London, 1949, p. 240.

a small city — say Elizabethan London with its eighty or ninety thousand inhabitants. What happens to existing societies when they are brought into such intimate contact by press, picture stories, news-reels and jet propulsion? What happens when the neolithic Eskimo is compelled to share the time and space arrangements of technological man? What happens in our minds as we become familiar with the diversity of human cultures which have come into existence under innumerable circumstances, historical and geographical? Is not what happens comparable to that social revolution which we call the American melting-pot?

When the telegraph made possible a daily cross-section of the globe transferred to the page of newsprint, we already had our mental melting-pot for cosmic man — the world citizen. The mere format of the page of newsprint was more revolutionary in its intellectual and emotional consequences than anything that could be *said* about any part of the globe.

When we juxtapose news items from Tokio, London, New York, Chile, Africa and New Zealand we are not just manipulating space. The events so brought together belong to cultures widely separated in time. The modern world abridges all historical times as readily as it reduces space. Every*where* and every *age* have become *here* and *now*. History has been abolished by our new media. If prehistoric man is simply preliterate man living in a timeless world of seasonal recurrence, may not posthistoric man find himself in a similar situation? May not the upshot of our technology be the awakening from the historically conditioned nightmare of the past into a timeless present? Historic man may turn out to have been literate man. An episode.

Robert Redfield in his recent book *The Primitive World and its Transformations* points to the timeless character of preliterate societies where exclusively oral communication ensures intimacy, homogeneity and fixity of social experience. It is the advent of writing that sets in motion the urban revolution. Writing breaks up the fixity and homogeneity of preliterate societies. Writing creates that inner dialogue or dialectic, that psychic withdrawal which makes possible the reflexive analysis of thought via the stasis of the audible made spatial. Writing is the translation of the audible into the spatial as reading is the reverse of this reciprocal process. And the complex shuttling of eye, ear and speech factors once engaged in this ballet necessarily reshape the entire communal life, both inner and outer, creating not only the 'stream of consciousness' rediscovered by contemporary art, but ensuring multiple impediments to the activities of perception and recall.

So far as writing is the spatializing and arrest of oral speech, however, it implies that further command of space made possible by the written message and its attendant road system. With writing, therefore, comes logical analysis and specialism, but also militarism and bureaucracy. And with writing comes the break in that direct, intuitive relationship between men and their surroundings which modern art has begun to uncover.

'Compared with the evidence afforded by living tradition,' says Sir James Frazer, 'the testimony of ancient books on the subject of the early religion is worth very little. For literature accelerates the advance of thought at a rate which leaves the slow progress of opinion by word of mouth at an immeasurable distance behind. Two or three generations of literature may do more to change thought than two or three thousand years of traditional life.'[2] But literature, as we know today, is a relatively conservative time-binding medium compared with press, radio and movie. So the thought is now beginning to occur: How many thousands of years of change can we afford every ten years? May not a spot of culture-lag here and there in the great time-flux prove to be a kind of social and psychological oasis?

Involved with the loss of memory and the psychic withdrawal of alphabetic cultures, there is a decline of sensuous perception and adequacy of social responsiveness. The preternatural sensuous faculties of Sherlock Holmes or the modern sleuth are simply those of preliterate man who can retain the details of a hundred-mile trail as easily as a movie camera can record it. Today our detailed knowledge of societies existing within the oral tradition enables us to estimate accurately the advantages and disadvantages of writing. Without writing there is little control of space, but perfect control of accumulated experience. The misunderstandings of Ireland and England can be seen in some basic respects as the clash of oral and written cultures. And the strange thing to us is that the written culture has very little historical sense. The English could never remember; the Irish could never forget. Today the university as a community is in large degree one in which the members are in regular oral communication. And whereas the university has a highly developed time sense, the business community operates on the very short-run and exists mainly by the control of space. The present divorce between these two worlds is only accentuated by the perfection of the media peculiar to each.

---

2 J. Frazer, *Man, God and Immortality*, 1927, p. 318.

Faced with the consequence of writing, Plato notes in the *Phaedrus*:

> This discovery of yours will create forgetfulness in the learners' souls, because they will not use their memories; they will trust to the external written characters and not remember of themselves. The specific which you have discovered is an aid not to memory, but to reminiscence and you give your disciples not truth but only the semblance of truth; they will be hearers of many things and have learned nothing; they will appear to be omniscient and will generally know nothing; they will be tiresome company, having the show of wisdom without the reality.

Two thousand years of manuscript culture lay ahead of the Western world when Plato made this observation. But nobody has yet studied the rise and decline of Greece in terms of the change from oral to written culture. Patrick Geddes said that the road destroyed the Greek city-state. But writing made the road possible, just as printing was later to pay for the roads of England and America.

In order to understand the printed-book culture which today is yielding, after four hundred years, to the impact of visual and auditory media, it is helpful to note a few of the characteristics of that manuscript culture which persisted from the 5th century b.c. to the 15th century a.d. I shall merely mention a few of the principal observations of scholars like Pierce Butler and H. J. Chaytor. In the first place, manuscript culture never made a sharp break with oral speech because everybody read manuscripts aloud. Swift, silent reading came with the macadamized surfaces of the printed page. Manuscript readers memorized most of what they read since in the nature of things they had to carry their learning with them. Fewness of manuscripts and difficulty of access made for utterly different habits of mind with regard to what was written. One result was encyclopedism. Men of learning tried, at least, to learn everything. So that if learning was oral, teaching was even more so. Solitary learning and study came only with the printed page. And today when learning and study are switching more and more to the seminar, the round-table and the discussion group, we have to note these developments as due to the decline of the printed page as the dominant art form.

The manuscript page was a very flexible affair. It was not only in close rapport with the oral speech but with plastic design and colour illustration. So the ornate examples of manuscript art easily rival and resemble those books in stone and glass, the cathedrals and abbeys. In our own time James Joyce, seeking a means to orchestrate and control the various verbi-voco-visual media of our own age, resorted to the page format of the *Book of Kells* as a means thereto. And even the early romantic poets, painters and novelists expressed their preference for gothic in terms of rebellion against book culture.

Recently Rosamund Tuve in elucidating the art of George Herbert discovered that the characteristic effects of metaphysical wit in the 17 th century poetry resulted from the translation of visual effects from medieval manuscript and woodcut into the more abstract form of the printed word. If the 17 th century was receding from a visual, plastic culture towards an abstract literary culture, today we seem to be receding from an abstract book culture towards a highly sensuous, plastic pictorial culture. Recent poets have used simultaneously effects from both extremes to achieve witty results not unlike those of the 17 th century. The impact of Mr. Eliot's very first lines of poetry has been felt everywhere:

Let us go then, you and I,
When the evening is spread out against the sky
Like a patient etherized upon a table.

It is the overlayering of perspectives, the simultaneous use of two kinds of space which creates the shock of dislocation here. For if all art is a contrived trap for the attention, all art and all language are techniques for looking at one situation through another one.

The printed page is a 16 th century art form which obliterated two thousand years of manuscript culture in a few decades. Yet it is hard for us to see the printed page or any other current medium except in contrast to some other form. The mechanical clock, for example, created a wholly artificial image of time as a uniform linear structure. This artificial form gradually changed habits of work, feeling and thought which are only being rejected today. We know that in our own lives each event exists in its own time. Time is not the same for the speaker as for the audience. To the speaker it is too, too brief for what he has to say. For the audience it is grim foretaste of eternity. Ultimately the medieval clock made Newtonian physics possible. It may also have initiated those orderly linear habits which made possible the rectilinear page of print created from moveable type, as well as the methods of commerce. At any rate the mechanization of writing was as revolutionary in its consequences as the mechanization of time. And this, quite apart from thoughts or ideas conveyed by the printed page. Moveable type was already the modern assembly line in embryo.

Harold Innis explored some of the consequences of the printed page: the break-down of international communication; the impetus given to nationalism by the commercial exploitation of vernaculars; the loss of contact between writers and audience; the depressing effect on music, architecture and the plastic arts.

Bela Balazs in his *Theory of the Film* notes some of the changes in visual habits resulting from the printing press on one hand and the camera on the other:

> The discovery of printing gradually rendered illegible the faces of men. So much could be read from paper that the method of conveying meaning by facial expression fell into desuetude. Victor Hugo wrote once that the printed book took over the part played by the cathedral in the Middle Ages and became the carrier of the spirit of the people. But the thousands of books tore the one spirit . . . into thousands of opinions . . . tore the church into a thousand books. The visual spirit was thus turned into a legible spirit and visual culture into a culture of concepts. . . . But we paid little attention to the fact that, in conformity with this, the face of individual men, their foreheads, their eyes, their mouths, had also of necessity and quite correctly to suffer a change.
>
> At present a new discovery, a new machine is at work to turn the attention of men back to a visual culture and to give them new faces. This machine is the cinematographic camera. Like the printing press it is a technical device for the multiplication and distribution of products of the human spirit; its effect on human culture will not be less than that of the printing press. . . . The gestures of visual man are not intended to convey concepts which can be expressed in

words, but such . . . non-rational emotions which would still remain unexpressed when everything that can be told has been told. . . . Just as our musical experiences cannot be expressed in rationalized concepts, what appears on the face and in facial expression is a spiritual experience which is rendered immediately visible without the intermediary of words.

The printed page in rendering the language of the face and gesture illegible has also caused the abstract media of printed words to become the main bridge for the inter-awareness of spiritual and mental states. In the epoch of print and word culture the body ceased to have much expressive value and the human spirit became audible but invisible. The camera eye has reversed this process in reacquainting the masses of men once more with the grammar of gesture. Today commerce has channeled much of this change along sex lines. But even there the power of the camera eye to change physical attitudes and make-up is familiar to all. In the 90's Oscar Wilde noted how the pale, long-necked consumptive red-heads painted by Rosetti and Burne-Jones were for a short time an exotic visual experience. But soon in every London salon these creatures sprouted up where none had been before. The fact that human nature, at least, imitates art is too obvious to labour. But the fact that with modern technology the entire material of the globe as well as the thoughts and feelings of its human inhabitants have become the matter of art and of man's factive intelligence means that there is no more nature. At least there is no more external nature. Everything from politics to bottle-feeding, global landscape, and the subconscious of the infant is subject to the manipulation of conscious artistic control — the BBC carries the unrehearsed voice of the nightingale to the Congo, the Eskimo sits entranced by hill-billy music from West Tennessee. Under these conditions the activities of Senator McCarthy belong with the adventures of the Pickwick Club and our talk about the Iron Curtain is a convenient smoke-screen likely to divert our attention from much greater problems. The Russians differ from us in being much more aware of the non-commercial impact of the new media. We have been so hypnotized with the commercial and entertainment qualities of press, radio, movie and TV that we have been blind to the revolutionary character of these toys. The Russians after a few years of playing with these radio-active toys have tried to neutralize them by imposing various stereotypes on their content and messages. They have forced their press to stick to an 1850 format. They have imposed similar time-locks on music and literature. They hope, thereby, to abate the revolutionary fury of these instruments. But the fury for change is in the form and not the message of these new media, a fact which seems almost inevitably to escape men trained in our abstract literary culture. The culture of print has rendered people extremely insensitive to the language and meaning of spatial forms — one reason for the architectural and city horrors tolerated by predominantly book cultures. Thus the English and American cultures in particular were overwhelmed by print, since in the 16 th century they had only rudimentary defences to set up against the new printed word. The rest of Europe, richer in plastic and oral culture, was less blitzed by the printing press. And the Orient has so far had many kinds of resistance to offer. But the curious thing is that Spaniards like Picasso or Salvador Dali are much more at home amidst the new visual culture of North America than we ourselves.

This division between visual and literary languages is a fact which has also set a great abyss between science and the humanities. Thinking as we do of culture in book terms, we are unable to read the language of technological forms. And since our earliest esthetic responses are to such forms, this has set up numerous cleavages between official and idiomatic cultural response within our own experience. We are all of us persons of divided and sub-divided sensibility through failure to recognize the multiple languages with which our world speaks to us. Above all it is the multiplicity of messages with which we are hourly bombarded by our environment that renders us ineffectual. Karl Deutsch has argued that a people shaped by oral tradition will respond to an alien challenge like a suicidal torpedo. The wild Celtic charge. A people shaped by a written tradition will not charge, but drift, pulled in a thousand different directions.

One obvious feature of the printed book is its republicanism. The page of print is not only a leveller of other forms of expression; it is a social leveller as well. Anyone who can read has at least the illusion of associating on equal terms with anyone who has written. And that fact gave the printed word a privileged place in American society and politics. The Duke of Gloucester could say casually to Edward Gibbon, on the completion of his *History*: "Another damned fat square book. Scribble, scribble, scribble, eh, Mr. Gibbon!" But there were no fox-hunters in America to put the literary upstart in his place.

So far as quantity goes the printed took was the first instrument of mass culture. Erasmus was the first to see its meaning and turned his genius to the manufacture of textbooks for the classroom. He saw, above all, that the printing press was a device for reproducing the past in the present, much like a Hollywood movie set. The nouveaux riches of Italy began to enact on a tiny scale the past that was being unearthed and printed. Hastily they ran up villas and palazzas in ancient style. Assisted by the newly printed exemplars they began to imitate the language of Cicero and Seneca. In England the new print mingled with the old oral tradition to produce the new forms of sermon and drama which were hybrids of written and spoken culture. But in the printing press there is one great feature of mass culture which is lacking. Namely, the instantaneous. From one point of view, language itself is the greatest of all mass media. The spoken word instantly evokes not only some recently conceived idea but reverberates with the total history of its own experience with man. We may be oblivious of such overtones as of the spectrum of colour in a lump of coal. But the poet by exact rhythmic adjustment can flood our consciousness with this knowledge. The artist is older than the fish.

Reading the history of the newspaper retrospectively we can see that it was not a mere extension of the art form of the book page. As used by Rimbaud, Mallarmé and Joyce the newspaper page is a revolution in itself, juxtaposing many book pages on a single sheet. And the news page was, moreover, more nearly a mass medium not only in reaching more people than the book but in being more instantaneous in its coverage and communication. Once linked to the telegraph, the press achieved the speed of light, as radio and TV have done since then. Total global coverage in space, instantaneity in time. Those are the two basic characters that I can detect in a mechanical mass medium. There are other characteristics derivative from these, namely anonymity of those originating the messages or forms, and anonymity in the recipients. But in respect of this anonymity it is necessary to regard not only words and metaphors as mass media but buildings and cities as well.

The modern newspaper page is not a mere extension of the book page because the speed with which the telegraph feeds news to the press today precludes any possibility of organizing a sheet of news by any but the most impressionistic devices. Each item lives in its own kind of space totally discontinuous from all other items. A particularly vigorous item will sprout a headline and provide a kind of aura or theme for surrounding items. So that, if the book page could imitate visual perspective as in Renaissance painting setting facts and concepts in proportions that reproduced the optical image of the three-dimensional object-world, the uninhibited world of the press and modern advertising abandoned such realistic proprieties in favour of weighting news and commercial objects by every dynamic and structural device of size and colour bringing words and pictures back into a plastic and meaningful connection. If the book page tends to perspective, the news page tends to cubism and surrealism. So that every page of newspapers and magazines, like every section of our cities, is a jungle of multiple, simultaneous perspectives which make the world of hot-jazz and be-bop seem relatively sedate and classical. Our intellectual world, by virtue of the same proliferation of books (over 18,000 new titles in England alone last year) has achieved the same entanglement which is easier to assess through the complexity of our visual environment. It is not just a quantitative problem, of course. As Gyorgy Kepes states it in his *Language of Vision*:

The environment of man living today has a complexity which cannot be compared with any environment of any previous age. The skyscrapers,

> the street with its kaleidoscopic vibration of colors, the window-displays with their multiple mirroring images, the street cars and motor cars, produce a dynamic simultaneity of visual impression which cannot be perceived in the terms of inherited visual habits. In this optical turmoil the fixed objects appear utterly insufficient as the measuring tape of the events. The artificial light, the flashing of electric bulbs, and the mobile game of the many new types of light-sources bombard man with kinetic colour sensations having a keyboard never before experienced. Man, the spectator, is himself more mobile than ever before. He rides in streetcars, motorcars, and aeroplanes and his own motion gives to optical impacts a tempo far beyond the threshold of a clear object-perception. The machine man operates adds its own demand for a new way of seeing. The complicated interactions of its mechanical parts cannot be conceived in a static way; they must be perceived by understanding of their movements. The motion picture, television, and, in a great degree, the radio, require a new thinking, i.e., seeing, that takes into account qualities of change, interpenetration and simultaneity.

That situation can be snapshotted from many angles. But it always adds up to the need to discover means for translating the experience of one medium or one culture into another, of translating Confucius into Western terms and Kant into Eastern terms. Of seeing our old literary culture in the new plastic terms in order to enable it to become a constitutive part of the new culture created by the orchestral voices and gestures of new media. Of seeing that modern physics and painting and poetry speak a common language and of acquiring that language at once in order that our world may possess consciously the coherence that it really has in latency, and which for lack of our recognition has created not new orchestral harmonies but mere noise.

Perhaps the terrifying thing about the new media for most of us is their inevitable evocation of irrational response. The irrational has become the major dimension of experience in our world. And yet this is a mere by-product of the instantaneous character in communication. It can be brought under rational control. It is the perfection of the means which have so far defeated the end, and removed the time necessary for assimilation and reflection. We are now compelled to develop new techniques of perception and judgment, new ways of reading the languages of our environment with its multiplicity of cultures and disciplines. And these needs are not just desperate remedies but roads to unimagined cultural enrichment.

All the types of linear approach to situations past, present or future are useless. Already in the sciences there is recognition of the need for a unified field theory which would enable scientists to use one continuous set of terms by way of relating the various scientific universes. Thus the basic requirement of any system of communication is that it be circular, with, of course, the possibility of self-correction. That is why presumably the human dialogue is and must ever be the basic form of all civilization. For the dialogue compels each participant to see and recreate his own vision through another sensibility. And the radical imperfection in mechanical media is that they are not circular. So far they have become one-way affairs with audience research taking the place of the genuine human vision, heckling and response. There is not only the anonymity of press, movies and radio but also the factor of scale. The individual cannot discuss a problem with a huge, mindless bureaucracy like a movie studio or a radio corporation. On the other hand a figure like Roosevelt could mobilize the networks for a war with the press. He could even make the microphone more effective by having the press against him, because the intimacy of the microphone preserved his human dimension while the national scale of the press attack could only appear as a tank corps converging on a telephone booth.

Thus the microphone invites chat, not oratory. It is a new art form which transforms all the existing relations between speakers and their audiences and speakers and their material of discourse. 'The great rhetorical tradition which begins with Halifax and runs through Pitt to Channing, sent up its expiring flash in Macaulay. [3] The modern manner was less declamatory and more closely reasoned. And the new manner which Gladstone handled like a Tenth Muse was based on facts and figures. Statistics represents a branch of pictorial expression. If the rise of bureaucracy and finance changed the style of public and private speech, how much more radical a change is daily worked in our habits of thought and discourse by the microphone and the loudspeaker.

Perhaps we could sum up our problem by saying that technological man must betake himself to visual metaphor in contriving a new unified language for the multiverse of cultures of the entire globe. All language or expression is metaphorical because metaphor is the seeing of one situation through another one. Right on the beam. I'll take a rain check on that.

One's vernacular is best seen and felt through another tongue. And for us, at least, society is only appreciated by comparing and contrasting it with others. Pictorial and other experience today is filled with metaphors from all the cultures of the globe. Whereas

---

3 G. M. Young, *Victorian England*, 1944, p. 31.

the written vernaculars have always locked men up within their own cultural monad, the language of technological man, while drawing on all the cultures of the world, will necessarily prefer those media which are least national. The language of visual form is, therefore, one which lies to hand as an unused Esperanto at everybody's command. The language of vision has already been adopted in the pictograms of scientific formula and logistics. These ideograms transcend national barriers as easily as Chaplin or Disney and would seem to have no rivals as the cultural base for cosmic man.

H. M. McLuhan

Culture without Literacy
Marshall McLuhan - Unbound (06)

ISBN: 1-58423-051-7
Library of Congress Control Number 2005927213

Marshall McLuhan Unbound Project Editors
Eric McLuhan, W. Terrence Gordon

Published in United States in October 2005 by
Gingko Press, Inc.
5768 Paradise Drive, Suite J · Corte Madera, CA 94925
(415) 924-9615 · Fax (415) 924-9608
email: books@gingkopress.com
http://www.gingkopress.com

Design, packaging and production: Die Gestalten Verlag, Berlin
Layout and Typography: onlab, Berlin
Fonts: *Dolly* by Underware, *Bullet* by House Industries
Production: Martin Bretschneider, Vinzenz Geppert
Art direction: Robert Klanten

Made in Germany